Countdown to
C·H·R·I·S·T·M·A·S

Advent Thoughts, Prayers, and Activities

by Susan Heyboer O'Keefe

Illustrated by Christopher Fay

Paulist Press

New York / Mahwah, N.J.

LIBRARY OF CONGRESS CATALOGING-IN-PUBLICATION DATA

O'Keefe, Susan Heyboer.
    Countdown to Christmas : Advent thoughts, prayers, and activities / Susan Heyboer O'Keefe ; illustrated by Christopher Fay.
       p.   cm.
    Summary: A collection of daily scripture readings, meditations, prayers, and activities for Advent and Christmas.
    ISBN 0-8091-6628-3 (alk. paper)
    1. Advent—Prayer-books and devotions—English—Juvenile literature.   2. Christmas—Prayer-books and devotions—English—Juvenile literature.   3. Children—Prayer-books and devotions—English—Juvenile literature.   4. Activity programs in Christian education—Juvenile literature.   [1. Advent—Prayer books and devotions.   2. Christmas—Prayer books and devotions. 3. Prayer books and devotions.]   I. Fay, Christopher L., ill. II. Title.
BV40.O34   1995
242'.33—dc20
                               95-16257
                                  CIP
                                  AC

Published by Paulist Press
997 Macarthur Boulevard
Mahwah, New Jersey 07430

Design: Christine Taylor
Composition: Wilsted & Taylor Publishing Services

Printed and bound in the United States of America

*For my son Daniel,
who helped me regain
the true meaning of Christmas*

♣

*With special thanks to
Mount Carmel School
Tenafly, New Jersey*

and

*St. Bartholomew School
Scotch Plains, New Jersey*

Whoever you live with is your family.

Introduction

This book will help you celebrate Advent and Christmas. Though Christmas is always on December 25, sometimes Advent begins in November and sometimes in December. To keep things simple and to let you use this book *every* year, *Countdown to Christmas* starts on December 1. It continues day by day until January 6, the traditional end of the Christmas season. Each day has a scripture quote, a few thoughts on the quote, a short prayer, then a Christmas activity for you to do alone or with your family.

When the word "family" is used in this book, it means every type of family you could find. *Your* family might include a dozen brothers or sisters, or none; two parents, one parent, or none; stepbrothers or sisters; half-brothers or sisters; stepparents, birth parents, adoptive parents, foster parents; grandparents, aunts, uncles, cousins, or friends. Whoever you live with is your family. Whoever you love, even if he or she is not there, is also your family.

To use this book, read the pages for the day, then let them be a jumping-off point for your own ideas. Perhaps the scripture quote will mean something different to you. Or perhaps an activity will help you think up one of your own. When that happens, it becomes a way of celebrating that's truly unique to you and your family!

In the wilderness prepare the way of the Lord,
make straight in the desert a highway for our God.

ISAIAH 40:3

Advent is a time of preparation. We should prepare both ourselves and our world for Jesus' coming. This doesn't mean preparing for the holiday by shopping, decorating, and cooking. While these things are enjoyable, it's more important that we prepare ourselves spiritually, that we make ourselves ready.

Are we ready for Jesus to come? What must we do to get ready? A book of meditations and activities like this one is a start. What else can you do to get ready for Christmas?

Dear Lord, I want to prepare myself for your coming.
Help me keep my thoughts on you and not on gifts or
other treats. Help me understand what I must do to get ready.

F · I · R · S · T

Start with an Advent Wreath

If you don't have an Advent wreath, it's not too late to make one yourself. A simple wreath can be made using four identical candle-holders arranged in a square about 8″ to 10″ on each side. Place small evergreen branches—real or artificial—between the candle-holders. For the candles, choose three purple candles and one pink. Light the first purple candle every night, then light the others in this order: a second purple candle starting on the second Sunday in Advent, the pink candle starting on the third Sunday in Advent, and the final purple candle starting on the last Sunday in Advent. Now all four candles will be lit. Each night, say Advent prayers or grace before meals after lighting the candles. You can even make up a prayer for your own special situation. For example: "Lord, let this Advent candle shine on Dad and Joe, who couldn't be here with us tonight, and let its light guide them home safely. Amen."

Therefore the Lord himself will give you a sign.
Behold, a young woman shall conceive and bear a son,
and shall call his name Immanuel.

ISAIAH 7:14

Sometimes it feels as though God is very, very far away from us. We want proof that he's here. We want signs and miracles.

But we already have signs and miracles all around us at every moment: there is no greater miracle than life itself. Each one of us—including you—is a miracle! The hard part is to be able to see the miracle in people who don't see it in themselves, like a pesky brother or step-sister or the class bully. If you look very hard, you'll see it. And if you see it, maybe they will, too.

God, help me to see the miracle in each person, even when he or
she is unfriendly or mean. Though I may not see it,
each person is really a sign from you, a true miracle.
Let me recognize the miracles around me.

S · E · C · O · N · D

Each of us—including you—is a miracle!

Do a good deed a day—like washing dishes.

Be a Guardian Angel

For the Christmas season, do a good deed a day—but secretly. For example, fold the laundry or wash dishes when no one is looking.

Some families put everyone's name in a hat and each person picks a name. Then all season long you have to do good deeds or dream up little surprises for just that one person—but without getting caught. On Christmas morning everyone reveals whose angel he or she was.

D · E · C · E · M · B · E · R

Repent, for the kingdom of heaven is at hand.

MATTHEW 3:2

When we think of repentance, we usually think of Lent. Advent is also a time for repenting. Sorrow is a way to prepare ourselves for Jesus' coming. We must feel sorry before we can make changes in our behavior. We've been waiting for the Lord for so long. It's easy to think our sins may have kept him away.

But Jesus comes to us despite our sins. That is how much he loves each of us. He took on our human form just to be closer to us. He became like us to help show how we can become like him.

Jesus, I want to be like you. Help me to
make changes in my life and to feel your love for everyone.

T · H · I · R · D

We must feel sorry before we can make changes in our behavior.

Drop the fifty cents into the can instead.

Make a Kringle Can

At the beginning of Lent your church, school, or Sunday School may give you a little can to collect money. At the end of Lent, whatever you've put into the can is donated to charity.

Make a "Kringle Can" to serve the same purpose during Advent. Decorate a coffee can or anything else with a plastic lid, using wrapping paper, glitter, or plain paper with your own Christmas designs. Have someone older cut a slit in the plastic lid, big enough to drop coins through. Then the next time you have spare change, drop it in the can. Want a candy bar? Drop the fifty cents into the can instead. Remember—Advent is also a time of repentance. When the Christmas season is over, donate the contents of your Kringle Can to a special charity or the poor box at church.

D · E · C · E · M · B · E · R

Say to those who are of a fearful heart,
"Be strong, fear not! Behold your God will come. . . ."

ISAIAH 35:4

Do you know how powerful you are? Every word that comes from your mouth has the power to hurt or to help. With a word you can tear someone down or you can give that person strength. You can make the person afraid or help get rid of that fear. Like a king or a queen, you should use your power wisely.

Dear God, help me to use my powers wisely
so I can make people feel better, rather than worse.
Let me offer strength and encouragement, just as you
always strengthen and encourage me.

F · O · U · R · T · H

"My, what an exceptionally *cold, wet nose you have!"*

Try to praise at least one person a day.

Surprise Someone with the Gift of Praise

Praise is a gift that costs nothing but a few seconds. Yet it can give the listener a wonderful boost for hours. What kind of things could you say? Tell your brother he's having "a good hair day." Tell a friend how impressed you are by his or her test result. Tell your Dad or stepfather how good the dinner he made tasted. Tell Grandma how many compliments you've had on the sweater she knitted you. Think of praise as a good deed and try to praise at least one person each day.

D · E · C · E · M · B · E · R

The desert shall rejoice and blossom;
like the crocus it shall blossom abundantly.

ISAIAH 35:1–2

"The desert shall rejoice and blossom." What a miracle—the dry lifeless desert filled with flowers! This is exactly what a miracle is: something happens that is totally opposite of what you expect. But wait a minute, you may say. The desert *does* blossom. Even cacti produce flowers. The desert *isn't* lifeless; it only looks lifeless. In a way, the miracle is already there. We simply have to open our eyes to it and to the many other miracles of life.

The second part of the quote echoes this thought. The desert shall bloom abundantly like the crocus, a flower that appears in early spring. Yet the crocus is so tiny. Sometimes we have to look hard to find it among the blades of grass. And sometimes we have to look hard for the miracles already present in our lives.

God, never let me stop looking for the miracles in life.
They are always there, waiting to surprise and encourage me.
Help me to keep my eyes and my heart open at all times.

F · I · F · T · H

Even cacti produce flowers.

Celebrate the Miracle of Family and Friends

Let others know the good news your family has to tell. Have your whole family write one long letter to send to all those friends and relatives you won't be able to see over the holidays. Let each member of your family write his or her own section. Then photocopy the letter and mail it out to those on your Christmas card list.

If you can't write a family letter, write a "good news" letter for your friends instead. Send it to anyone you won't be seeing over the holidays—friends who'll be away, that boy you met in summer camp, that girl from the visiting basketball team, or a favorite teacher who moved away.

D · E · C · E · M · B · E · R

Come to me all who labor and are heavy laden,
and I will give you rest.

MATTHEW 11:28

Jesus offers help to all people. Sometimes he works directly through miracles. Many times he works through others, such as St. Nicholas, a bishop in the fourth century who performed acts of charity and was the inspiration for Santa Claus.

Let Jesus work through *you* this Advent season. Open your heart to his word. Listen to what he's telling you to do. Just as you can see Christ in others, you should *be* Christ-like so that others can see him reflected in you.

It's not easy to be like you, Lord, but I want to try.
Help me to hear your voice above the loud noises
of the season and to understand what it is you want me to do.

S · I · X · T · H

"St. Nick" and *Ralph: "Me, too, please."*

Play Santa Claus

Gather up your old toys and clothes that are still in good condition and give them away. Here are some suggested places: the Salvation Army, the children's ward of a local hospital, a foster home, or a holiday sale run by a church, a synagogue, or a town organization.

Don't be afraid that you have nothing to give: the most precious gift of all is always your time. Volunteer at a hospital or a nursing home to read to the patients. Or join an "adopt a grandparent" program and be matched up with someone who would love company, especially at this time of year. You can send this person drawings, letters, or your home-baked cookies . . . talk to him or her on the phone . . . or even visit. If there's no formal "adoption" program in your neighborhood, look around for an elderly neighbor who lives alone and who might need cheering up for the holiday.

D · E · C · E · M · B · E · R

Welcome one another, therefore,
as Christ has welcomed you. . . .

ROMANS 15:7

How does Christ welcome us? With full acceptance, no matter who we are or what we've done. We know we should accept others the same way, but it's sometimes very difficult. How can we welcome people we don't like?

Many of the people we don't like may be relatives we see only once or twice a year, including Christmas. Even though they are family, they seem more like strangers. Make the effort to welcome them or they will remain strangers to us forever.

Lord, you love me always. No matter what I've done,
you are always ready to welcome me back
into your love. Help me to accept others the same way—
to welcome them, to love them, as you would.

S · E · V · E · N · T · H

How can we welcome people we don't like?

"Make Room" at the Inn

You may be having company staying at your house for the holidays—a grandparent or an aunt or uncle. In the room where the company will stay, completely clean out a dresser drawer so this person can use it while visiting. Also add a few things he or she might like or could use. You could put in a pocket-sized copy of the Psalms, some candy, a mystery to read at night, stationery to write letters, or a new pair of slippers.

And Mary said, "Behold, I am the handmaid of the Lord;
let it be done to me according to your word."

LUKE 1:38

Mary said *yes* to God with her whole heart. She couldn't foresee that saying *yes* meant she would lose her son to a horrible death. But she said *yes* anyway, willingly accepted the unknown, and helped bring salvation to the world.

We, too, must learn to say *yes* to God, no matter what happens. Like Jesus' death, the results of saying *yes* may be hard, confusing, even painful. But we must hold on to the sure knowledge that God's plan eventually leads us to the joy of the resurrection.

How do I say "yes" to you, God? It's just so scary.
You ask people to do difficult things, things I'm not sure I can do.
Help me to learn to trust you. It's a first step to saying "yes."

How can I say yes to you, God? It's just so scary.

Give the Miracle of Life

"Adopt" a baby by helping a poor child overseas through one of the many monthly support programs. Your monthly check brings that child the basics of food, clothing, and shelter. If you and your family can't afford this, maybe your class, school, or church can chip in for the "adoption."

If none of these is possible, ask your church or local foster-child agency if there's a special child to whom you could give a Christmas gift. The church or agency will pass the gift along anonymously.

The house of the Lord shall be established. . . .
Nation shall not lift up sword against nation,
neither shall they learn war anymore.

ISAIAH 2:2,4

Jesus came to us as proof of God's love and forgiveness. That makes Christmas a good time for us to express our love and heal our hurts. We've already "learned war"—how to argue and call names and make fun of others. Now it's time to stop and make peace.

God, help us to learn peace and to
settle things without anyone getting hurt.

N · I · N · T · H

Write a note saying that you want to be friends again.

Heal the Hurts

During the Christmas season everyone seems to feel a little friendlier toward others. Take advantage of this spirit to forgive someone who hurt you or to apologize to someone you may have hurt. If it's too hard to say the words, write a note to the person saying that you want to be friends again.

D · E · C · E · M · B · E · R

The Lord says: "Keep justice and do righteousness, for soon my salvation will come, and my deliverance be revealed."

ISAIAH 56:1

We're so used to getting presents every holiday that we forget they're a luxury. In fact, we almost think of them as a necessity. How terrible we feel if we don't get exactly what we want.

For some people Christmas presents truly *are* a luxury—a luxury they cannot afford because they are struggling to give their families the real necessities of food, clothing, and shelter. We need to keep our eyes open to this reality so we can "do the right thing."

God, I want to be aware of what other people need this Christmas, not just what I want. Show me the ways I can help.

T · E · N · T · H

Go through your kitchen closet and put together a bag of groceries . . .

Feed the Hungry

With your parents' permission, go through your kitchen closet and put together a bag or box of groceries to donate to a food center for the hungry. Choose foods that don't need refrigeration—like peanut butter, pasta, soup, or cereal. If you can, include holiday food such as cranberry sauce, instant stuffing, or pie crust and canned pie filling.

If your family can't spare any groceries, give the food center a few hours of your time instead. Help re-stock shelves, babysit the children of the volunteers, or stuff envelopes in the center's office. There are lots of things you can do!

D · E · C · E · M · B · E · R

Now hope that is seen is not hope.
For who hopes for what he sees?
But if we hope for what we do not see,
we wait for it with patience.

ROMANS 8:24–25

God gives us so many things; one thing he asks in return is that we believe, that we have hope and faith in him. We have not seen God. We have not seen Jesus. Yet we are asked to believe in what we haven't seen. Even more, we are asked to wait in patience. All this is the very nature of hope and belief.

Perhaps that's why we celebrate Advent and Christmas each year. The season is a time of waiting and hoping, followed by the fulfillment of our hope, the birth of Jesus. Jesus does not live among us physically as he did two thousand years ago. But celebrating each Christmas makes his presence here today a little more real—and helps us wait for him with a little more hope.

Lord, I believe in you; help my unbelief.

E · L · E · V · E · N · T · H

Help Others Hope

Many relatives or close friends may not be able to see you this Christmas, yet they hope to see you soon. Here is a great gift for anyone who is not able to share in this year's celebrations.

Get a plain calendar for the new year. Mark down in color all important family days for the year—birthdays, expected births, wedding dates, anniversaries, graduations, etc. Paste family photos wherever there's space. Then when friends or relatives look at the calendar, they will find a hint of what they hope to soon see.

If you have no family member who'd like a "hope" calendar, make one for yourself. Using old magazines, paste up pictures of places you'd like to visit, people you'd like to meet, careers you'd like to try. Each picture is your own hope for the future.

D · E · C · E · M · B · E · R

May the Lord make you increase and
abound in love to one another and to all. . . .

1 THESSALONIANS 3:12

"Increase in love to one another and to all. . . ." Love is more than words. Love is also more than how we feel. Words can lie, and feelings change from day to day. To truly love, we must back up our words and our feelings with loving actions. When we wish we hadn't said something or when we're in a bad mood, our actions can still "love" for us.

Lord, when my lips are shut and my heart is closed,
let my hands continue to work in love.

T · W · E · L · F · T · H

Hide a note where a family member is sure to find it.

Hide an "Angel" Note

Remember the second day's activity where you became a "guardian angel" for someone? Write and hide a note where a family member is sure to find it—like a briefcase or a lunchbox. Tell that person why he or she is special, or simply say "I love you." If you're shy about saying something like this, don't sign your name. Just write that this has been a "Note from an Angel."

*According to his promise we wait for a new heaven
and a new earth in which righteousness dwells.*

2 PETER 3:13

Each year we wait for Jesus to come again to us through the miracle of Christmas. But, in a way, we're also waiting for his second coming when he will bring us a new heaven and a new earth. Each Christmas we find personal renewal; we can let God make each one of us a new person. God will also renew heaven and earth, creating for us a perfect place where his peace and justice are complete and will last forever.

*Lord, let me help you prepare your perfect place
by doing what is right. Help me bring peace where
there is argument, and justice where there is injustice.*

T · H · I · R · T · E · E · N · T · H

Make a Christmas ornament to put on your tree.

Count Your Years of Happiness

Each year that we hope for God's perfect place is a year of waiting. But in that waiting there are also many moments of happiness, especially with friends and family at Christmas. Mark the time with a new annual celebration: each year make a Christmas ornament to put on the tree. (Make extras to give away as gifts.) Some suggestions for handmade ornaments are paper snowflakes, tiny boxes wrapped in paper and bows, or a small photograph of yourself pasted onto cardboard and "framed" with wrapping-paper. A fancier ornament is a decorated egg. Here's how to make one:

Use a pin to carefully make a small hole about ⅛" big on both ends of an egg. Poke the pin around inside from the bottom to break the yolk, then press your lips to one hole and blow—hard! Keep blowing till nothing more comes out. Save the inside of the egg to eat. (A good time to try this is when you're going to use several eggs anyway, say, to scramble or to add to a cake. That's because the shells are so fragile you may end up with a broken shell for every one that stays whole.) Rinse out the empty egg, let it dry overnight, then decorate it with metallic paint, glitter, or sequins. Glue a loop on top to hang from the tree.

No matter what kind of ornament you make, each one creates a happy memory.

The wolf shall dwell with the lamb, and the
leopard shall lie down with the baby goat . . .
and a little child shall lead them.

ISAIAH 11:6

Christmas is a time of healing our hurts so that opposites or even enemies can find peace. The wolf and the leopard shall sleep peacefully with the lamb and the baby goat, instead of feasting on them. These different animals may represent warring nations or just individuals who don't get along. Whoever they are, it's a little child—the Christ child—that leads them and shows them the way.

You, too, can be "the little child" who shows others the way to peace. Peace-making is not a job just for adults. In fact, too many adults have forgotten an important lesson of their childhoods: when you argue, apologize quickly. It's the only way to hold onto friends and to keep people who aren't friends from turning into enemies.

This season, show by your own example how to make peace.

Lord, sometimes I don't want to heal hurts. I'd rather see
my enemies just disappear. Soften my heart and help me
to make the same peace that you offer to everyone equally.

F · O · U · R · T · E · E · N · T · H

Or—tell your story entirely with illustrations.

Make Your Own Book

Write and illustrate your own book to keep or to give away. Make up a story, write down a favorite family memory, or copy down your favorite poem or story by someone else. Handwrite the words or use a typewriter or a computer to type them. Leave space on some or all of the pages for your own illustrations, or for pictures from magazines or comics.

Some of the best books contain no words at all. If you want, tell your story entirely with illustrations and other pictures.

Whether or not your book uses words, create a cover out of construction paper or poster board and decorate it with drawings, paint, glitter, stickers—whatever you want. The cover will not only make your book fancier; it will help protect your beautiful work.

The grass withers, the flower fades;
but the Word of our God will stand forever.

ISAIAH 40:8

Christmas will be here before you know it, the presents will be opened, the excitement will be over—and then what? It's easy to feel let down and to think, "Is that all there is?"

This year remember that Christmas is about Jesus coming to live among us. After all the fuss of gift-giving is over, he remains with us every day and forever. He's not like the toy that breaks the first time you use it or the video game that gets boring once you've beaten it. As God's greatest gift, he will never fail you, never leave you, never stop loving you.

Dear God, help me to understand that the
true meaning of Christmas is Jesus—and that he
comes to us every single day throughout the year.

Give each person an I.O.U. gift as well.

Dream Up I.O.U. Gifts

Whether you're going to make or buy gifts for your family, give each person an "I.O.U. gift" as well. What is it? Think of a favor you could do for each person. Maybe you could rub Dad's neck, wash the dishes when it's your sister's turn, or teach your younger brother how to ride a bike. Write your favor in fancy letters, put it in an envelope marked with the person's name, and put the envelope under the tree.

The Lord has taken away the judgments against you . . .
he will rejoice over you with gladness;
he will renew you with his love. . . .

ZEPHANIAH 3:15,17

What might we expect from a God who takes away all judgments against us; in other words, a God who forgives all our sins? If we think in human terms, we might expect from time to time a reminder of how "bad" we were and how "good" God was to forgive us. We might even expect God to have some doubts about us in the future.

But God does not have these human weaknesses. He doesn't react with doubt. Instead, after forgiving us our sins, he rejoices over us with gladness and renews us with his love. How? He shows his love in the greatest possible way by sending his son to become one of us.

Lord, help me to forgive the people I think have
harmed me in some way. Then help me to truly forget
and to follow forgiveness with love.

S · I · X · T · E · E · N · T · H

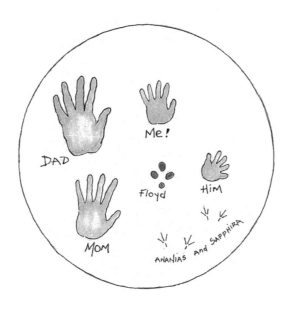

Give Your Family a Hand of Love

Here's a special way to see your family's love for each other. Ask each person to trace his or her hand onto a piece of paper. You do it, too. Cut each paper hand out and use it as a pattern to cut two copies from fancy material. Sew the two copies together inside out, leaving the wrist open. Turn the material right side out, stuff it, then sew the wrist closed, too.

When you have a stuffed hand for every person in your family, hang them up as ornaments. Or else use them to create a "hand mobile." Either way you can see all the hands of your family reaching out for each other.

The hand mobile is also a great project for a school or religion class, a dormitory, a club, or even a sports team to try. Everyone needs a hand from time to time! The mobile is a good reminder of how many people are always waiting to help you.

I am the Lord your God, who teaches you to profit,
who leads you in the way you should go.

ISAIAH 48:17

There are so many different paths in life we can take— different ways to talk and act and have fun, different friends to pick, different decisions to make at every moment. Should we cheat on this test, or risk failing? Should we ignore that person, or say hello? Should we skip church, or go with the hope that we will hear something meaningful today?

Where should we look for help? Sometimes we feel we can't talk to our parents, and sometimes our friends are just as confused as we are. Scripture says God will "lead us in the way we should go." That means step by step, minute by minute—not just during special times like Advent and Christmas, but every ordinary day. Where else could we find such reliable help?

Lord, I think I'll feel funny asking you if I should be friends with
someone or what to do on a test. But that's what
my days are like and I want you to be part of them. Help me
to turn to you more frequently and to listen to what you say.

S · E · V · E · N · T · E · E · N · T · H

You can also help your teacher.

Clean for the Holidays

Help your parents get ready for the holidays. You can start by cleaning your own room. Then do something else, such as polishing the silverware, bringing the tree lights or ornaments out of the dusty basement, or putting clean sheets on the guestroom bed.

You can also help your teacher get ready for the holidays. Start with straightening out your own desk, then volunteer to wash the blackboard, sweep or dust, or help decorate the class.

And don't forget your church! Ask your minister or priest what you can do to help prepare for Christmas.

D · E · C · E · M · B · E · R

"Behold, the days are coming," says the Lord,
"when I will fulfill the promise."

JEREMIAH 33:14

In one way Christmas is very strange. Jesus is already here, yet we eagerly wait for his coming all over again. Perhaps that's why Christmas is also a time of renewal, an opportunity to start over. Just as Jesus is "born again" year after year, so we have endless chances to start over, make changes, try again.

Making changes and starting over means repentance. That's why the priest or minister wears purple for most of Advent; purple is the color of repentance. But too often repentance is thought of as a gloomy time. Who wants that? Instead, think of it as a huge eraser that helps get rid of those things in the past you'd like to forget or do over. Advent gives you a clean start. Begin your new life today.

God, each day you give me a chance at a new life.
Help me do what I must to begin again—whether
I need to forgive, to forget, to change, to love more,
to be less afraid. With your son's help I can do anything.

E · I · G · H · T · E · E · N · T · H

Draw your own Nativity scene.

Set Up Your Christmas Stable

Begin to set up the nativity scene or crèche. You can set it up all at once today. Another way to set up the stable emphasizes that this is a time of waiting; add only one or two pieces every day to the stable until Christmas morning, when you finally add the infant Jesus. If you have a younger brother or sister, ask if he or she would like to help.

If your family doesn't have a crèche, draw your own nativity scene. To emphasize that this is a time of waiting, draw just one or two figures each day until you've completed the picture.

D · E · C · E · M · B · E · R

For the mountains may depart and the hills be removed,
but my steadfast love shall not depart from you. . . .

ISAIAH 54:10

God's love for us is eternal and unchanging. It doesn't matter what we do or what is happening around us. God loves us whether we've been obedient or disobedient. God loves us whether our day is calm or the very earth is being torn apart through floods, tornados, or earthquakes. God does not wish such bad things on us. When they happen, he offers us enough love to help us through—no matter how badly or how angry we feel at the time.

At Christmas, we see the greatest proof of God's love; he sent his son to become one of us, to become fully human in all ways but sin. Jesus is God's love for us. Welcome him into your hearts.

Lord, there are many days when I don't feel loving or lovable.
Help me to remember that your love doesn't change with moods
even though mine may. Help me to reach out for your love every
day, and especially when I need it most.

N · I · N · E · T · E · E · N · T · H

Lord, there are many days when I don't feel loving or lovable.

Make Gift Tags

Gifts are just one expression of our love for each other. To make your gifts a little more special, make your own gift tags. Use last year's Christmas cards or leftover cards from the ones your parents sent this year. Cut the picture side of the card into little squares. Punch a hole into one corner using a hole punch, then tie a ribbon through the hole. Write the person's name on the white side of the card and tape the ribbon to the package.

But you, O Bethlehem, who are little to be
among the clans of Judah, from you shall come forth
for me one who is to be ruler in Israel. . . .

MICAH 5:2

Never overlook the small or the meek or the boring or the routine as unimportant. That boy or girl in your class who never talks may actually be one of the most interesting people you'll ever know. That routine chore you do for your stepmother may actually help hold the whole house together. Those dull prayers you say every night may actually create the path to God you'll need someday during a crisis. And one of the tiniest towns in all of Judah was actually the birth-place of the savior.

Lord, I, too, am considered little in this world,
almost invisible, because I'm not yet grown up.
Remind others of my importance and just how much
I can do; and remind ME not to overlook the other
"little ones" who live almost invisibly around me.

T · W · E · N · T · I · E · T · H

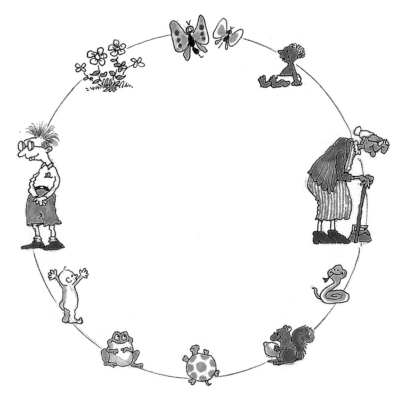

Remind me not to overlook the other "little ones"
who live almost invisibly around me.

Decorate Your Own Wrapping Paper

With your own artwork, plain white or brown paper becomes even more special than the most expensive wrapping. Use crayons, water color, or magic markers to decorate plain white or brown paper, or even brown grocery bags. Don't use tempera or other heavy paint as it may crack when the paper is folded around a gift. Draw Christmas scenes or colorful abstracts. You could write "Merry Christmas" or the person's name over and over in different colors and fancy letters to make a design of its own.

D · E · C · E · M · B · E · R

And Hannah said, "For this child I prayed; and the Lord has granted me my petition which I made to him. Therefore I have lent the child to the Lord; as long as he lives, he is lent to the Lord."

I SAMUEL 1:27

Year after year Hannah was unable to have a child. Finally she went to the temple. She cried and prayed and promised that if she could have a child, she would give him back to the Lord by entering him in the priesthood. God answered her prayers. He said she would give birth and she did. She named the child Samuel and handed him over to the temple. When Samuel grew up, he became a great prophet.

Hannah is how *we* should be as a covenant people of God. We prayed to God to send us a savior. In return we promised God ourselves—our love and our loyalty. Now Jesus is here. Have we kept our part of the covenant?

Lord, I want to keep my promises to you—from the promises my parents made for me during baptism, to personal promises I make to you on my own. You never let me down. Help me to do the same.

T · W · E · N · T · Y · F · I · R · S · T

Give a Gift to Jesus

Jesus is the fulfillment of God's promise to us. Because Jesus was fully human, Christmas is not just the day he first appeared; it's his birthday. What can you give Jesus as a birthday gift? Here are some examples:

You could be a "peacemaker" and try to settle arguments between classmates, instead of just watching them fight. You could let your stepsister watch her favorite T. V. shows for a week. You could cooperate when your parents ask you to do something. You could memorize a new scripture quote each day.

If you promise Jesus something for his birthday, do your best to keep your promise. And don't give up if you forget one day: just try again the next.

Rejoice always, pray constantly, give thanks in all circumstances;
for this is the will of God in Christ Jesus for you.

I THESSALONIANS 5:16–18

Rejoice, pray, be thankful. It's easy to be happy during the Christmas season as we anticipate the coming celebration. It's easy to pray every day around the Advent wreath. It's easy to be thankful when we see how much we have now and how much more we'll receive for Christmas.

But scripture says, "Rejoice *always*, pray *constantly*, give thanks *in all circumstances*." It would be wonderful to learn how to do these three things every day: during the rainy spring, the hot sticky summer, the bare grey autumn—whether you passed a test or failed a test, whether you're with friends or all alone.

Lord, your glory and power are all around me every day,
not just holidays. Every day, whether good or bad, help me
to praise your goodness and to thank you for all I have.

T·W·E·N·T·Y · S·E·C·O·N·D

Share Your Holiday

If you know of a friend or neighbor who will be spending the holiday alone, ask your parents if he or she can come over on Christmas Eve or Christmas Day. Even just an hour or two with your family can be the best present this person receives.

If you can't invite this person over or if he or she can't get around, there are other ways you can share the holiday. Perhaps you could send over some food, anything from home-baked cookies to a hot holiday meal. Or perhaps you could get a group together to sing carols outside his or her house. Even just leaving a candy cane on this person's doorstep or in the mailbox can provide a pleasant surprise.

Or perhaps you could sing carols outside of his or her house.

. . . the Lord whom you seek will suddenly come to his temple. . . . But who can endure the day of his coming, and who can stand when he appears?

MALACHI 3:1–2

Advent scripture often talks about waiting: be ready, be alert, but be patient, because we never know when the Lord will come. Today's quote says the Lord will come "suddenly," perhaps when we don't expect him. But it adds something else: God is so great and powerful, who will have the strength to even stand in his presence?

Perhaps that is one reason why Jesus came to us not just as another human, but as the most helpless human—a baby. Jesus was born just as we were. Like us, he grew and learned and doubted and suffered. There were days he was happy, days he was sad, days he felt lonely, days he perhaps even felt he was a failure—just as we sometimes do. He understands all that we go through because he lived through it himself.

Lord, you experienced life the way I do. Let me always remember your humanity so that I'll learn to turn to you like a best friend or a loving brother or sister when I need help.

T · W · E · N · T · Y · T · H · I · R · D

Make a birthday cake for Jesus.

Bake a Birthday Cake for Jesus

Celebrate the humanity of Jesus once again. The other day you gave him a special gift for his birthday. Now bake him a birthday cake or buy one ready-made that you can then share with family or friends. Write "Happy Birthday, Jesus" on it and ask a grown-up to help you light one candle. Let your youngest brother or sister (or the youngest person in the room) make a wish and blow the candle out.

Christmas Eve

For the grace of God has appeared for the salvation of all people.

TITUS 2:11

Christmas should be a time of union, of coming together with all people in peace. Too often it becomes a time when we note the many differences between people. One family may give inexpensive gifts while another gives lavish presents. This person won't come because he or she isn't speaking to that person. And for many reasons, some people don't celebrate Christmas at all.

But Jesus, the grace of God, appeared for the salvation of *all* people. Instead of looking for the differences that separate us, remember that love unites us all, now at Christmas, and always.

Lord, help me to ignore the differences that separate me
from others this year—including the difference between what
I want and what I receive. I have all that I need in your love.
Let your love guide me to others in peace.

T · W · E · N · T · Y · F · O · U · R · T · H

Have your family and friends act out the Nativity scene.

Put on a Christmas Play

Have the whole family or a group of your friends join in to act out the nativity or other Christmas scene. There are plenty of parts—the Holy Family, the innkeeper, angels, shepherds, and Wise Men—and everyone already knows what to do and say. (For a quick reminder, take a look at Chapter 2 of Luke.) Use towels, sheets, and blankets to make "old-fashioned" robes. And if anyone has the use of recording equipment, make an audio or a video tape of the play to send to relatives or friends who couldn't join you.

D · E · C · E · M · B · E · R

Christmas

And the word became flesh and dwelt among us.

JOHN 1:14

The word of God is his promise. His promise was made flesh in Jesus. What of our own words, our own promises? Do we "give them flesh" by turning our promises into actions? If God had not made his word flesh, we would not have been saved. What happens when we don't fulfill our promises?

God, help me to make no promise that I cannot keep
and to keep those promises I've already made.

T · W · E · N · T · Y ‑ F · I · F · T · H

Read the Gospel before opening presents.

Read the Nativity Gospel

Whether you've already gone to church or are planning to go later today, it's good to hear the gospel again in your own home. Read the Christmas gospel of how God kept his word to us, before opening presents. Or, if your brothers or sisters can't wait, read it out loud when everyone sits down together for breakfast. A good scripture selection for today is Luke 2:1–14.

Lord, now let thy servant depart in peace, according to thy word;
for mine eyes have seen thy salvation. . . .

LUKE 2:29–30

The words above were spoken by Simeon, an old man who had
been promised by God that he would not die till he had seen Israel's
savior. Mary and Joseph had brought the infant Jesus to the temple.
Just the sight of the baby inspired Simeon's words and allowed him
to die in peace.

This same kind of joyful trust can help us live in peace. We can
pass every day with the sure knowledge that God has kept his promise, and that we are loved and saved.

Lord, give me the peace of Simeon to live every day of my life.
And when I can, help me to pass that peace onto others.

Cook Up Family Memories

You may or may not cook, but you probably love to eat special holiday treats relatives prepare. While everyone is still together, make a
family cookbook. Let each person share a recipe for his or her favorite food, as well as a little story about it when possible. For example,

T · W · E · N · T · Y · S · I · X · T · H

Ralph's FAVORIT
Recipee

HuGe RAW T-BONE
STeaK
iN A
PUSSYCAT SAUCE
wit
SpArrow iN a
CHOCKLiT
Sauce Fer
Dessert

Make your own recipe book.

perhaps Grandpa's uncle brought one recipe with him from over-seas. Or perhaps the first time Mom tried her recipe, it exploded in the oven. Write up the recipes and stories, then make as many pho-tocopies of each as the number of books you want to make.

To turn the recipes into a book, paste each recipe onto colored construction paper. Then use a 3-hole punch to make holes on the left-hand side of the paper. Make a cover by drawing a family picture or using, with your parents' permission, a copy of a family photo-graph. Punch 3 holes in that page, too. Now stack up the finished pages, string holiday ribbon through the holes, and tie the pages together. A masterpiece!

If you want, save the cookbooks till next Christmas to give as gifts.

*Jesus is the offering for our sins, and not for ours
only but also for the sins of the whole world.*

1 JOHN 2:2

Christmas is a good time to make up with family and friends because that's what Jesus did. He took on our sins and "healed the hurts" between ourselves and God. And he did this for everyone.

Many times we can accept this for other people, but not for ourselves. Somehow we can't say, can't really believe, "Jesus was born for *me*. He suffered for *me*. He died for *me*. And he rose so that *I* could share in his eternal life." Are we so wicked or so unimportant that even God couldn't possibly include *us*, personally, in his plan? Not true. God's love is for all of us, together, but it's also for each one of us as individuals.

*Lord, help me to understand that you love me just the way I
am right now and that Jesus was born for me as I am right now.
Teach me this special love so that I in turn can learn to love others.*

Write Thank-You Notes

We have so many reasons to thank the people in our life. Spend today writing thank-you notes. Say why you liked the gift and how you will use it. Also thank these people for being themselves. If someone did not give you a gift, but helped make your holiday special, write a thank-you note anyway. That person gave you just as much as the other people.

Sometimes words are very hard to put in writing even when we know what we want to say. In this case, you may want to make your own cards: your artwork becomes the thank-you itself.

To make your own notes, fold a sheet of typing or computer paper in half, then in half again. Decorate the cover with crayon or marker drawings. You could also use a hole punch on construction paper to create lots of colored circles. Paste several of these on the cover, draw a straight line down from each, and you have a bunch of balloons. Another way to decorate your notes is to dip a sponge into paint or ink, then lightly dab the sponge all over the paper to create a design. (You may want to practice on scrap paper first.) Inside your home-made note, simply write "Thank you"—once, or over and over. Use fancy letters if you wish.

When you've finished, write a thank-you note to Jesus as well for being the proof of God's love for you.

Go and tell. . . what you hear and see:
the blind receive their sight and the lame walk, lepers are
cleansed and the deaf hear, and the dead are raised up,
and the poor have good news preached to them.

MATTHEW 11:4–5

Christmas is a time of miracles, though often not the kind you hoped for. Did you get that new video game system you wanted? Now *that* would have been a miracle! you say. Maybe, but there are greater miracles—like making up with a relative you argued with or turning an enemy into a friend. These would be much greater than anything you could hold in your hands, yet they're within your power. You may not be successful, or you may be successful and never know it, but *your* action, all alone, is a miracle in itself.

Lord, turn me into a miracle-maker, a peace-maker,
this Christmas season and all year long.

T · W · E · N · T · Y · E · I · G · H · T · H

Give a Wish Gift

Sometimes you don't get to see friends and relatives until after Christmas is over. What a nice surprise to find there are still gifts waiting to be opened.

Make a miracle by giving each person in your family and each of your friends a final gift, a "wish gift"—the thing you'd like to give most, no matter what it is. What does that person really need? Courage? Hope? Good health? A four-year scholarship? Have everyone write down what his or her "wish gift" is for every other person, then share all your wishes out loud. These wishes are miracles of love.

Have everyone write down a "wish gift" for everyone else.

This is the message we have heard from him and proclaim to you,
that God is light and in him is no darkness at all.

1 JOHN 1:5

Everyone loves a story with a happy ending. That's why the story of God's love for us is so compelling; it shows us that in God there is no darkness, no hatred, no vengeance, no death. In God there is only light, love, forgiveness, and life everlasting.

When we try to live on our own, without God's help, life may feel like a "choose your own adventure" book—all alone as we pass through trouble after trouble, the possibility of a bad end at any flip of the page. That's not the life God wants for us. He wants to be with us, chapter by chapter, helping us through our troubles, always guiding us toward an end that folds us into his love.

God, the ending you want for me is filled with peace
and happiness. But sometimes there seem to be too
many troubles between where I am and where you want
me to be. Help me to take your hand with trust and let you
guide me through the darkness to your light.

T · W · E · N · T · Y · N · I · N · T · H

Read out loud while the other person is doing a chore.

Read Out Loud

People like all kinds of stories: true ones like the story of your faith, or a history or biography, or made-up stories like a short story or novel. Read one of your favorite stories out loud to a member of your family. Or if you received a book for Christmas, read from your new gift. Reading out loud while the other person is doing a chore, such as washing the dishes or shining shoes, will help the chore go faster.

Wives, be subject to your husbands, as is fitting in the Lord.
Husbands, love your wives and do not be harsh with them.
Children, obey your parents in everything, for this pleases the
Lord.

COLOSSIANS 3:18–20

What a picture scripture creates: family members loving and listening to each other in perfect peace, just as the Holy Family must have lived. Each person has a role in the family. Sometimes, because of absence or separation, we may have to fill the role of another person as well as our own role. But at heart each person—mother, father, stepmother, stepfather, child, stepchildren—knows the role he or she should take on. And love is always at the center of it.

Lord, help me to make and keep my family a perfect circle of love.
Whenever we fight or have trouble, help us all
to remember that our love for you and each other
should always be the center of our family life.

T · H · I · R · T · I · E · T · H

At the dinner table, tell everyone the best thing that happened to you, then the worst.

Share Around the Table

At the dinner table, tell everyone the best thing that happened to you today, then the worst. Now ask everyone else to share the best and worst that happened to him or her. How did each of you feel when these things happened?

D · E · C · E · M · B · E · R

New Year's Eve

*Watch, therefore, for you do not know
on what day your Lord is coming.*

MATTHEW 24:42

Watch and wait, for we don't know when the Lord is coming. This may seem like strange advice: Christmas is over. Yet Jesus is still coming to us—next Christmas, and the next, and at the end of time. The end of time? Surely we have long enough to get ready.

But Jesus also comes to us every day—in a friend's request or a stranger's need, a bowl of soup from Dad or an unexpected hug from a cousin. Will you recognize Jesus in all these disguises? The only way is to watch and be ready at all times. Soon we will learn to recognize Jesus in all people and during every minute of the day.

*Lord, it's so hard to be ready all the time. I try to prepare,
but I'm so easily distracted. Help me to always keep a part of
myself in silence, listening for your word, looking for your face.*

T · H · I · R · T · Y · F · I · R · S · T

Is there something you should stop doing?

Watch and Wait

Many people make "New Year's resolutions." A resolution is a promise to yourself to try to change behavior—either break bad habits or form good new habits. Sometimes a resolution is to accomplish something important.

Make a New Year's resolution to watch for Jesus. Learn to see him in yourself. Learn to see him in others. Is there something you should stop doing, like making fun of someone, or *start* doing, like praying more often, that will help you "see" Jesus better? Write it down and make this your big goal for the New Year.

New Year's Day

But Mary kept all these things, pondering them in her heart.

LUKE 2:19

What happiness, awe, fear, and confusion Mary must have felt about the events of the past few days. She'd miraculously given birth to a baby. Then shepherds told her they had seen angels filling the sky, proclaiming her son to be the savior. What did it mean? She asked no one, but "kept all these things" in her heart and wondered about them.

Sometimes we also see, hear, and experience things we do not talk about. These things may seem too strange or wonderful for words, or too painful to tell. So we think about them in silence. But in our hearts, in the middle of the silence, is God, always ready to listen, the one who truly understands all our thoughts.

Lord, you are always there, eagerly listening to my every word.
Help me to talk to you more often and to quiet all my
racing thoughts so I can hear you whispering back.

F · I · R · S · T

Create a Box of Memories

One thing we often think about in our hearts is our memories. Begin to hold onto good memories right now. Find a box with a lid—a cigar box, shoe box, or clothing box. Decorate it with paint, colored paper, wrapping paper, or leftover Christmas cards.

Over the coming months fill the box with things that are important to you: letters, souvenirs, ticket stubs, photos, awards, and so on. Next New Year's Day you will have a very interesting collection to go through. Each item will be a wonderful memory.

Beloved, if God so loved us, we also ought to love one another.

1 JOHN 4:11

God is perfect love. He puts no conditions on his love; he loves us now and always, just the way we are this very minute. He loves us those days we don't love him back; he loves us even when we're convinced we're unlovable.

We should try to imitate God's accepting love with all people. That doesn't mean we should agree with or do everything others do. Even God is displeased when we sin. But he always looks beyond the action to the person and he always loves the person.

Lord, whenever someone does something that hurts me,
let me see beyond the action. Let me see the person as
you do so I can feel forgiveness, acceptance, and love.

Start a Group Journal

Love often grows deeper with understanding. Here's a way to create better understanding among the people you live with.

Get everyone—whether it's just you and your grandmother or a whole dormitory of roommates—to "collect their feelings" day by

S · E · C · O · N · D

You could also leave messages for each other....

day. How? Put a brand-new notebook and pen in the living room. Then tell everyone to write down his or her feelings every day, sharing what happened and what it felt like. You could also leave messages for each other, things you'd like your stepfather or your sister or your roommate to know that may be too difficult to say out loud. The journal will help pull everyone closer together during the year. Then next New Year's you can read the journal together and see how far you've all come.

*. . . And taking the five loaves and the two fish Jesus
looked up to heaven, and blessed, and broke the loaves. . . .
And they all ate and were satisfied. And they took up
twelve baskets full of broken pieces and of the fish.
And those who ate the loaves were five thousand. . . .*

MARK 6:41–44

From five loaves and two fish Jesus fed the five thousand and the crowds were not only satisfied, they had leftovers! This is the kind of abundance that God promises each of us—not only to fill our needs, but to give us more than we need.

Sometimes we confuse needs with wants and think that God isn't listening. We won't wait trustingly. We want to do things *our* way and at *our* speed; when we're disappointed, we blame it on God. If we could only learn to wait for him, we would receive his abundance.

*God, the miracles of your abundance are all around me unseen.
Help me to be patient, to wait when I must, so I can
recognize and receive the many gifts you have for me.*

T · H · I · R · D

The Abundance of Your Family

Many times the old and the young are ignored, even when they're family members. Find out today the many riches they have to share with you. Pick the oldest person in your family, perhaps a grandparent, great-grandparent, or great aunt or uncle. If the person doesn't live nearby, get permission to call. Ask that person what his or her favorite Christmas memory is. Maybe it happened just this year. Then share what *your* favorite memory is. Now have the youngest person in your family share his or her best Christmas. Then share yours, too.

When the apostles saw Jesus walking on the sea they thought it was
a ghost and they cried out; for they all saw him and were terrified.
But immediately he spoke to them and said,
"Take heart, it is I; have no fear."

MARK 6:49–50

What a comfort Jesus' words must have been for the apostles. They were terrified! They thought that only a ghost, an evil spirit, could walk on the water. Then they heard that familiar voice say, "It is I; have no fear."

So often the unknown causes us to be afraid. It's why we don't like strangers or relatives we see only once a year: we simply don't know these people. But instead of remaining afraid we should try to discover who these people are. Then when we see them again, we won't be afraid; instead we will hear only a familiar voice.

Lord, each person has something important to reveal to me:
my neighbors, the kids at school I never talk to,
even my friends and my family—people I think I know.
Help me to be unafraid, to open myself up to others
so that all the voices I hear are familiar.

F · O · U · R · T · H

Find Out Who's Who

If the holiday photos have come back, put them into a photo album. Write a caption for each photo. If you can, go through older photos and label those as well. For older photos, have parents and relatives help you identify people you may not recognize. They're your family, too. Find out as much as you can about them.

Write a caption for each photo.

Behold, let us love one another; for love is of God,
and he who loves is born of God and knows God.

I JOHN 4:7

What should we remember most about Advent and the Christmas season? That it's a time of love. We show our love to friends and family through gifts and by sharing time with them. God showed his love for us in an even more special way by sending his only son to us as one of us—frail, mortal, human, and ready to die for us that we may live. There is no greater act of love.

Lord, show me how to love as you do—with full acceptance:
how to love myself, the people I'm close to, even those
I don't like or who have done me harm. Let me love people
I've never met and never will; and let me love your earth,
from each grain of sand, to each stinging bee.

F · I · F · T · H

Send a Letter of Love

Write a letter using words that encourage, uplift, and comfort. Tell the person that no matter where he or she is, there is always someone to watch over him, always someone thinking of her.

The letter should go to a person who doesn't live close by, a person you think may need encouragement—an uncle in the navy who may be homesick, a cousin in Asia whom you've never met. Before you seal the envelope, add this P.S.: "After you've read this letter, copy it over or write your own and send it to a person who might need encouragement right now."

Maybe your letter can create a chain of love that will someday criss-cross the entire world.

J · A · N · U · A · R · Y

Epiphany or "Little Christmas"

And lo, the star which the wise men had seen in the East went
before them, till it came to rest over the place where the child
was. . . and going into the house they saw the child with
Mary his mother, and they fell down and worshipped him.
Then opening their treasures, they offered him gifts,
gold and frankincense and myrrh.

MATTHEW 2:9–11

For most of us Epiphany is the end of the Christmas season. It's called "Little Christmas" because, although *our* gift-giving is over, it's the day the three Wise Men brought gifts to Jesus.

All these gifts are just small reminders of the gifts Jesus brought to us. We celebrate his first gift at Christmas, that he loved us so much he became one of us. In a few months we'll celebrate the gift of Easter, that Jesus died for us and rose from the dead so that we might have salvation and eternal life.

Lord, Christmas is over and Easter is months away.
Help me see that all the days between are also holidays
and holy days, because each one brings me closer to you.

S · I · X · T · H

Continue the Season!

Today is the traditional day to take down the tree. If you had a live tree, wreath, or branches, snip off a few large twigs and put them in water. They will last a long time, perhaps even into Lent.

Another way to link the two seasons is to have someone cut you two branches from the tree, one shorter than the other, and put a notch in each branch. The shorter branch should be notched at the halfway point; the longer branch at a third from the top. Now it's your turn: tie the branches together at the notches with purple yarn or ribbon. You'll have a cross to carry you into Lent.

What if your family's tree is artificial? Use leftover wrapping paper, cards, or ribbons to make your cross. For example, braid leftover ribbon; or make a mosaic by gluing small pieces of cut-up cards or wrapping onto cross-shaped cardboard. Display your cross till Easter, then save it as a decoration for next Christmas.

You'll have a cross to carry you into Lent.

Packing It Up

The Advent-and-Christmas season is less than two months long. All too soon, it seems, we're packing away the tree and decorations till next December. But though this book ends here, you can continue to use the pattern of its pages: every day read some scripture, think about what it means for you, then try to put your thoughts into an action or activity. These steps will help you keep a little Christmas in your heart every day of the year—and to see the dozens of miracles all around you that are just waiting to be discovered.